The Wind Was Rising
起风了

Na Ye 娜夜

translated by
Ouyang Yu 欧阳昱

PUNCHER & WATTMANN

First published in 2021
Published by Puncher and Wattmann
PO Box 279
Waratah NSW 2298

http://www.puncherandwattmann.com
puncherandwattmann@bigpond.com

NATIONAL
LIBRARY
OF AUSTRALIA

A catalogue entry for this book is available from the National Library of
Australia.

ISBN   9781925780628

Cover design and typesetting by Morgan Arnett
Printed by Lightning Source International

Contents

娜夜 女,满族,祖籍辽宁兴城。在西北成长。毕业于南京大学中文系。曾长期从事新闻媒体工作。现为专业作家。二十世纪八十年代中期开始诗歌写作。出版诗集《起风了》《睡前书》《个人简历》《神在我们喜欢的事物里》等。获第三届鲁迅文学奖,人民文学奖,十月文学奖,天问诗人奖,中宣部"四个一批"人才称号等。

An important and representative poet of contemporary Chinese women's poetry, Na Ye graduated from the Department of Chinese Language, Nanjing University. She began writing in 1985 and worked as a journalist for a long time and is now a professional writer and a member of China Writers Association based in Chongqing. Her poetry publications include *The Wind Was Rising*, *Written before I went to Sleep*, *C.V.*, and *God within the Things that We Like*. She has won The Third Lu Xun Literary Award (2005), People's Literature Prize (2007), October Literature Prize (2014) and Tian Wen Poets Prize (2011), as well as such titles as the One of the Top Ten Young Women Poets in the New Century and One of the Talented People in the 'Four Batches', awarded by the Ministry of Propaganda of China (2018). Her work has been translated into English, French, Japanese, Russian, German and Swedish. Her poetry is tinged by a sadness that originates from living itself, and is brave enough to stare at human limitations while reflecting the significance that the brevity of beauty could increase the value of beauty.

生活

我珍爱过你
像小时候珍爱一颗黑糖球
舔一口
马上用糖纸包上
再舔一口
舔得越来越慢
包得越来越快
现在　只剩下我和糖纸了
我必须忍住：忧伤

Life

I have treasured you

The way I treasured a black candy ball when I was little

Licking it

And wrapped it up with candy paper at once

I licked it again

But at a lower, and still lower speed

As I wrapped it up faster

Now   nothing is left except me and my candy paper

I have to bear it: sadness

起风了

起风了　我爱你　芦苇
野茫茫的一片
顺着风

在这遥远的地方　不需要
思想
只需要芦苇
顺着风

野茫茫的一片
像我们的爱　没有内容

The wind was rising

The wind was rising   I love you   the reeds
A vast wilderness
Along the wind

In such a faraway place   no need
For thoughts
All one needs is the reeds
Along the wind

A vast wilderness
Like our love   no contents

酒吧之歌

我静静地坐着　　来的人
静静地
坐着

抽烟
品茶
偶尔　望望窗外
望一望我们置身其中的生活

——我们都没有把它过好！

她是她弹断的那根琴弦
我是自己诗歌里不能发表的一句话

两个女人　　静静地　　坐着

The song of the bar

Quietly, I am sitting   the one who came
Is
Quietly sitting

Smoking
Sipping the tea
And, occasionally looking outside the window
Looking at the life in which we were located

—neither of us has lived it well!

She is the string of the instrument that she has broken
And I, a remark unpublishable in my own poetry

Two women   quietly   sitting

幸福

大雪落着　土地幸福
相爱的人走着
道路幸福

一个老人　用谷粒和网
得到了一只鸟
小鸟也幸福

光秃秃的树　　光秃秃的
树叶飞成了蝴蝶
花朵变成了果实
光秃秃地
幸福

一个孩子　　我看不见他
——还在母亲的身体里
母亲的笑
多幸福

——吹过雪花的风啊
你要把天下的孩子都吹得漂亮些

Happiness

A big snow falling   happy earth
People in love walking
Happy road

An old man   got a bird
With grains and a net
The little bird also happy

Bare trees   bare
Leaves turned into butterflies
Flowers turned into fruit
Barely
Happy

A child   I can't see him
—still inside his mother's body
Mother's smile
So happy

—the wind blowing across the snow-flowers
Please blow so all the kids under heaven are pretty

从酒吧出来

从酒吧出来
我点了一支烟
沿着黄河
一个人
我边走边抽
水向东去
风往北吹
我左脚的错误并没有得到右脚的及时纠正
腰　在飘
我知道
我已经醉了
这一天
我醉得山高水远
忽明忽暗
我以为我还会想起一个人
和其中的宿命
像从前那样
但　没有
一个人
边走边抽
我在想——
肉体比思想更诚实

Coming out of the bar

Coming out of the bar

I lit up a cigarette

Along the Yellow River

I, alone

Walked and smoked

The water ran east

The wind blew north

The mistakes made by my left foot were not corrected by my right foot in time

My waist   was drifting

I knew

I was drunk

That day

I got drunk like tall mountains and far waters

Light and dark

I thought I'd recall someone

And the fate within

Like before

But   no

Alone

I walked and smoked

And I was thinking—

Flesh was more honest than thought

在这苍茫的人世上

寒冷点燃什么
什么就是篝火

脆弱抓住什么
什么就破碎

女人宽恕什么
什么就是孩子

孩子的错误可以原谅
孩子　可以再错

我爱什么——在这苍茫的人世啊
什么就是我的宝贝

In this boundless world

Whatever coldness sets fire to
It is the bonfire

Whatever fragility grabs hold of
It breaks up

Whatever a woman forgives
It is a child

Mistakes by the child can be forgiven
The child   can keep making mistakes

Whatever I love—in this boundless world
It is my treasure

合影

不是你！是你身体里消失的少年在搂着我
是他白衬衫下那颗骄傲而纯洁的心
写在日记里的爱情
掉在图书馆阶梯上的书

在搂着我！是波罗的海弥漫的蔚蓝和波涛
被雨淋湿的落日　　无顶教堂
隐秘的钟声

和祈祷……是我日渐衰竭的想象力所能企及的
那些美好事物的神圣之光

当我叹息　　甚至是你身体里拒绝来到这个世界的婴儿
他的哭声
——对生和死的双重蔑视
在搂着我

——这里　　这叫做人世间的地方
孤独的人类
相互买卖
彼此忏悔

肉体的亲密并未使他们的精神相爱
这就是你写诗的理由？

一切艺术的源头……仿佛时间恢复了它的记忆
我看见我闭上的眼睛里
有一滴大海

A group photo

Not you! It's the disappearing teenager in your body that's holding me
It's his proud and pure heart underneath his white shirt
The love entered in a diary
The book dropped on the steps leading to the library

Holding me!   It's the blueness and the waves permeating in the Baltic Sea
The setting sun wetted by the rain the topless church
The mysterious sounds of the bells

And prayers…things that my gradually withering imagination could reach
And the sacred light of things beautiful

When I sigh   it's even the baby in your body that refuses to come to this world
His crying
—his double contempt for life and death
That is holding me

—here   in this place that is called the world
The solitary people
Are buying and selling
And mutually repenting

The intimacy of flesh has not made their spirits love
Or is that the reason for you to write poetry?

The source of all art   as if time had recovered its memory
I see in my closed eyes
A drop of ocean

在流淌

是它的波澜在搂着我！不是你
我拒绝的是这个时代
不是你和我

"无论我们谁先离开这个世界
对方都要写一首悼亡诗"

听我说：我来到这个世界就是为了向自己道歉的

Dripping

It's its wave that is holding me! Not you
What I have rejected is this age
Not you, not me

'Whoever first leaves this world
Must write an elegiac poem'

Listen: I've come to this world to apologize for myself

点赞

我为灵魂的存在和量子纠缠点赞
为暗物质和瓦楞上的无名草
为我书房里两只毛茸茸的鸟
在一幅画的山水中获得了永生
为空荡的监狱
成为被大地遗忘的石头
风沙变成芝麻
为我们这一代人
所经历的……
银杏叶飞舞着来世
成为金色蝴蝶的愿望
为重庆的太阳
但我有时又站在大雾一边
为这样的上帝：
要善待儿童和诗人
因为他们是我的使者……
在美国哈佛艺术馆
我为家乡的王道士
和流落在世界各博物馆的敦煌文物点赞
——在　就是好！

Praise

Praise the existence of soul and the entanglement of quantum

Praise dark matter and the nameless grass on the rooftiles

Praise the two fluffy birds in my study

that have acquired eternity in the mountains and waters of a painting

Praise an empty jail

for having turned into a stone, forgotten by the earth

the way wind and sands have turned into sesames

Praise this generation for what it has experienced…

the ginkgo leaves flying and dancing next life

and for their wish to become golden butterflies

Praise the sun in Chongqing

although I sometimes side with the big fog

Praise such a God:

Please treat kids and poets well

because they are my messengers…

in the Harvard Art Museums in America

I praised Monk Wang from my hometown

And the Dunhuang cultural relics, dispersed around world museums

—it's good as long as they are there

睡前书

我舍不得睡去
我舍不得这音乐　这摇椅　这荡漾的天光
佛教的蓝
我舍不得一个理想主义者
为之倾身的：虚无
这一阵一阵的微风　并不切实的
吹拂　仿佛杭州
仿佛正午的阿姆斯特丹　这一阵一阵的
恍惚
空
事实上
或者假设的：手——

第二个扣子解成需要　过来人
都懂
不懂的　解不开

Written before I went to sleep

I couldn't tear myself away and go to bed
Couldn't, from this music   this rocking chair   this ripply skylight
The Buddhist blue
Couldn't tear myself away from the nothingness
An idealist leans to
The breeze, ripple after ripple   is not real
Blowing   like Hangzhou
Like noon in Amsterdam   ripple after ripple
Trance-like
Empty
In fact
Or hypothetical: hands—

To be unbuttoned, the second button needs   someone in the know
All understandable
Those who don't understand   can't unbutton it

一首诗

它在那儿
它一直在那儿
在诗人没写出它之前　在人类黎明的
第一个早晨

而此刻
它选择了我的笔

它选择了忧郁　为少数人写作
以少
和慢
抵达的我

一首诗能干什么
成为谎言本身？

它放弃了谁
和谁　伟大的
或者即将伟大的　而署上了我——孤零零的
名字

A poem

It is there
It's been there
Before it's written by a poet   before the dawn of humanity
In the first morning

And at this moment
It has chosen my pen

It's chosen melancholy   to write for the few
The me
That can only be reached by few
By slow

What can a poem do?
To become the lie itself?

Who has it given up on?
And who   the great
Or the to-be great   with me signed on it instead—such a lonely
Name

青海青海

我们走了
天还在那儿蓝着

鹰　还在那儿飞着

油菜花还在那儿开着——
藏语大地上摇曳的黄金
佛光里的蜜

记忆还在那儿躺着——
明月几时有
你和我　缺氧　睡袋挨着睡袋

你递来一支沙龙：历史不能假设
我递去一支雪茄：时间不会重来

百年之后
人生的意义还在那儿躺着——
如果人生
有什么意义的话

Qinghai, Qinghai

We are gone
The sky still bluing there

The eagle   still flying there

The canola flowers still opening there—
The gold swaying in the land of Tibetan language
Honey in the light of Buddha

Memory still lying there—
When will we have the bright moon
You and I   a lack of oxygen   sleeping bag to sleeping bag

You passed a Salem to me: History is not hypothetical
I passed a cigar to you: Time won't return

In a century
Life's meaning still lies there—
If there is any meaning
In life at all

手语

两个哑孩子
在交谈　　在正午的山坡上

多么美　　太阳下他们已经开始发育的脸
空气中舞蹈着的：手
缠绕在指间的阳光　　风　　山涧溪水的回声
突然的
停顿
和
跳动
多么美

——如果　　没有脸上一直流淌的泪水……

Hand language

Two mute kids

Were talking   on the mountain slope at noon

So beautiful   their faces beginning to develop under the sun

Dancing in the air: the hands

The sunlight   the wind   the echoes of the mountain creeks, entwining

                             the fingers

A sudden

Pause

And

Jump

So beautiful

—if   there aren't tears that have been running nonstop down their faces…

十九楼

一根丝瓜藤从邻居的阳台向她午后的空虚伸来
它已经攀过铁条间的隔离带
抓紧了可靠的墙壁
二十一世纪　　植物们依然保持着大自然赋予的
美妙热情
而人心板结
荒漠化
厌世者也厌倦了自己
和生活教会她的……
十九楼
她俯身接住一根丝瓜藤带来的雨珠和黄昏时
有些哽咽：
你反对的
就是我反对的

On the nineteenth floor

A loofah vine extends itself from the neighbour's balcony to the emptiness
                                                    of her afternoon
having climbed over the belt of separation between the iron bars
and taking a tight grab of the reliable wall
in the twenty-first century   the plants still hold onto the beautiful
                                                    enthusiasm
Nature bestows on them
while the human hearts harden
becoming deserts
the misanthropist has grown weary of herself
and of what life has taught her...
on the nineteenth floor
when she leans to take the raindrops brought by the loofah vine and the
                                                    evening
she's choking up:
what you are against
is also what I'm against

没有比书房更好的去处

没有比书房更好的去处

猫咪享受着午睡
我享受着阅读带来的停顿

和书房里渐渐老去的人生

有时候　我也会读一本自己的书
都留在了纸上……

一些光留在了它的阴影里
另一些在它照亮的事物里

纸和笔
陡峭的内心与黎明前的霜……回答的
勇气
——只有这些时刻才是有价值的

我最好的诗篇都来自冬天的北方
最爱的人来自想象

No place better than the study

There's no place better than the study

Where my kitten is enjoying a nap
And I, enjoying a pause brought by my reading

And there is also the life that is ageing

Sometimes   I may also read a book of my own
All left on the paper...

Some lights are left in their own shadows
And others, in the things they are lighting up

Pen and paper
The steep heart and the pre-dawn frost...the courage
To reply
—only these moments are of value

My best poems come from the north in winter
And my best-loved people, from my imagination

喜悦

这古老的火焰多么值得信赖
这些有根带泥的土豆　白菜
这馒头上的热气
萝卜上的霜

在它们中间
我不再是自己的陌生人
生活也不在别处

我体验着佛经上说的：喜悦

围裙上的向日葵爱情般扭转着我的身体：
老太阳　你好吗？

像农耕时代一样好？
一缕炊烟的伤感涌出了谁的眼眶

老太阳
我不爱一个猛烈加速的时代
这些与世界接轨的房间……

朝露与汗水与呼啸山风的回声——我爱
一间农耕气息的厨房　和它
黄昏时的空酒瓶

小板凳上的我

Pleasure

The ancient flame is so trustworthy
These potatoes   bok choy   with mud and roots
The steam on this steamed bread
The frost on the turnip

Among them
I'm no longer a stranger to myself
And I no longer live elsewhere

I experience what is said in the Buddhist scriptures: pleasure

The sunflower on my apron, like love, twists my body:
Old sun   how are you going?

As good as in an agricultural era?
Sadness, like a wisp of chimney smoke, comes surging out of whose eyes

The old sun
I do not love a violently speeding age
These rooms that are connected, like rails, with the world...

Morning dew and sweat and echoes of the roaring mountain wind—I love
A kitchen smelling of farming   and its
Empty bottles at dusk

Me on a small stool

想兰州

想兰州
边走边想
一起写诗的朋友

想我们年轻时的酒量　热血　高原之上
那被时间之光擦亮的：庄重的欢乐
经久不息

痛苦是一只向天空解释着大地的鹰
保持一颗为美忧伤的心

入城的羊群
低矮的灯火

那颗让我写出了生活的黑糖球
想兰州

陪都　借你一段历史问候阳飓　人邻
重庆　借你一程风雨问候古马　叶舟
阿信　你在甘南还好吗！

谁在大雾中面朝故乡
谁就披着闪电越走越慢　老泪纵横

Missing Lanzhou

Missing Lanzhou
As I walk I miss
Friends who used to write poetry together with me

I miss our capacity for liquor when young   hot blood   on the plateau
Things polished bright by the light of time: solemn pleasure
Everlasting

Pain is an eagle that explains the earth to the sky
Keeping a heart sad for beauty

Sheep that have entered into the city
Lights that are low

The black candy ball that induced me to write about life
Missing Lanzhou

Peidu   I'll greet Yang Yang and Ren Lin   by borrowing a section of
your history
Chongqing   I'll greet Gu Ma and Ye Zhou   by borrowing a trip of your
wind and rain
Ah Xin   are you okay in south Gansu?!

Whoever faces his or her home in the big fog
Will walk the slower, shrouded in a lightning   tears running down the
face

这里……

没弄丢过我的小人书
没补过我的自行车胎
没给过我一张青春期的小纸条
没缝合过我熟得开裂的身体……这里
我对着灰蒙蒙的天空发呆　　上面
什么都没有　　什么都没有的天空
鹰会突然害怕起来　　低下头
有时我想哭　　我想念高原之上搬动着巨石般
大块云朵的天空　　强烈的紫外光
烘烤着敦煌的太阳　　也烘烤着辽阔的贫瘠与荒凉
我想念它的贫瘠！
我想念它的荒凉！
我又梦见了那只鹰　　当我梦见它
它就低下翅膀　　驮起我坠入深渊的噩梦
向上飞翔　　它就驮着我颤抖的尖叫
飞在平坦的天上——当我
梦见他！
这个城市不是我的呓语　　冷汗　　乳腺增生
镜片上的雾也不是　　它不是我渴望的：
同一条河流　　一个诗人床前的
地上霜　　我抬头想什么
它永远不知道　　它渐渐发白的黎明
从未看见我将手中沉默的烟灰弹进一张说谎的
嘴——它有着麦克风的形状
我更愿意想起：一朵朵喇叭花的山岗
和怀抱小羊的卓玛　　神的微笑
在继续……那一天
我醉得江山动摇　　那一天的草原

Here...

I've never lost my little-people books

I've never got my bicycle tires repaired

I've never received a slip of paper for my puberty period

I've never sewn together my body, ripe for ripping apart...here

I blankly stare at the grey sky   in it

There is nothing   in a sky with nothing

An eagle takes a sudden flight   and lowers its head

Sometimes I feel like crying   I miss the sky over the plateau that seems

To be moving rock-like clouds   strong ultraviolet light

The sun that is toasting Dunhuang   and the vast poverty and desolation

I miss its barrenness!

I miss its desolation!

I dream again of the eagle   when I dream of it

It lowers its wings   and carries me downwards into the nightmare of the abyss

Flying upwards   it carries my shivering shrieks

To fly over the plain sky—when I

Dream of him!

This city is not my raving   cold sweat   breast hyperplasia

Nor is the fog on the mirror   not the one I'm after:

The same river   before a poet's bed

The frost on the ground   it'll never know

What I'm thinking of when I raise my head the whitening dawn

Has never seen me flip the silent ash in my hand into a lying

Mouth—it's got the shape of a microphone

I prefer to think of: a hill of morning glories

And Zhuoma holding a lamb in her arms   the smile of a god

Continuing   the other day

I was so drunk the rivers and the mountains shook   the grassland that day

心中只有牛羊　　躺在它怀里
我伸出舌头舔着天上的星星：
在愿望还可以成为现实的古代……
黎明的视网膜上
一块又似烙铁的疤
当它开始愈合　　多么痒
它反复提醒着一个现场：人生如梦
你又能和谁相拥而泣
汉娜·阿伦特将一场道德审判变成了一堂哲学课
将她自己遗忘成一把倾听的椅子
失去故乡的拐杖……
人类忘记疼痛只需九秒钟
比一只企鹅更短
那颤抖的
已经停下
永不再来
只有遗忘的人生才能继续……这里
我栽种骆驼刺　　芨芨草　　栽种故乡这个词
抓起弥漫的雨雾
一把给阳关
一把被大风吹向河西走廊
而此刻　　我疲倦于这漫长的
永无休止的热浪　　和每天被它白白消耗掉的身体的激情

There were only cows and sheep in my heart   lying in their arms

I stuck out my tongue to lick the stars in the sky:

In the ancient times when wishes could turn into realities...

On the retina of dawn

Another scar that looked like an iron

When it began healing   so itchy

It kept reminding of a scene: life like a dream

Who can you hold and cry together

Hannah Arendt turned a moral trial into a class of philosophy

Forgetting herself till she turned into a listening chair

Losing the stick of home

It takes humanity nine seconds to forget the pain

Shorter than a penguin

The trembling

Has stopped

Never to return

Only the forgetful life can continue...here

I plant the camel thorn   Achyranthes splendens   planting the word of home

I grab hold of the pervasive rain fog

I'll give a handful to Yangguan

With another handful blown by the big wind to the Hexi Corridor

And, at the moment, I'm weary of this prolonged

Ceaseless heat wave   the passion of my body wasted by it in vain

移居重庆

越来越远……

好吧重庆

让我干燥的皮肤爱上你的潮湿

我习惯了荒凉与风沙的眼睛习惯你的青山绿水

法国梧桐

银杏树

你突然的电闪雷鸣

滴水的喧嚣

与起伏的平静

历史在这里高一脚低一脚的命运——它和我们人类

都没有明天的经验

和你大雾弥漫

天地混沌时

我抱紧双肩茫然四顾的自言自语：越来越远啊……

Migrating to Chongqing

Getting further away now...

All right, Chongqing

Let my dry skin fall in love with your moisture

My eyes, used to the desolation and wind and sand, have grown used to
                                        your green mountains and waters

The French plane-trees

The gingko trees

Your sudden flashes of lightning and thunder

Commotion of dripping water

And the heaving quietness

The fate of history, one step higher, one step lower here—it with us mankind

Having no experience of tomorrow

When together with your heavy fog

With heaven and earth merged in a chaos

I hold my shoulders, looking about me and talking to myself: getting
                                        further away...

写作

让我继续这样的写作：
一条殉情的鱼的快乐
是钩给它的疼

继续这样的交谈：
必须靠身体的介入
才能完成话语无力抵达的……

让我继续信赖一只猫的嗅觉：
当它把一些诗从我的书桌上
叼进废纸篓
把另一些
叼回我的书桌上

让我亲吻这句话：
我爱自己流泪时的双唇
因为它说过　我爱你
让我继续

女人的　　肉体的　　但是诗歌的：
我一面梳妆
一面感恩上苍
那些让我爱着时生出了贞操的爱情

让我继续这样的写作：
"我们是诗人——和贱民们押韵"
——茨维塔耶娃在她的时代
让我说出：

Writing

Let me carry on with writing like this:
The pleasure of a fish that has committed suicide for love
Is the pain the hook gives it

With talking like this:
One must reach what discourse can't
By the intervention of body...

Let me continue to trust the smell of a cat:
Let it take a number of poems from my desk
To the wastepaper basket
And bring another number of them
Back to my desk

Let me kiss this remark:
I love my lips in tears
Because they have said   I love you
Let me continue

The woman's   the body's   but the poetry's
As I make myself up
I thank God
And love that breeds chastity when I am in love

Let me carry on with writing like this:
'We are the poets—rhyming with the subalterns'
—Tsvetaeva in her age
Let me say it:

惊人的相似

啊呀——你来　你来
为这些文字压惊
压住纸页的抖

Amazing similarities

Ah—come, you, come
Help these words get over the shock
And press down the trembling paper

所有的

所有突然发生的……我都认定是你
一条空荡的大街
脸上的风
镜子里晃动的阳光
突然的白发
连续两天在上午九点飞进书房的蜜蜂
掉在地上的披肩
要走的人
和要走的神
心前区刺痛
划破我手指的利刃
包裹它的白纱布
继续渗出纱布的鲜血
所有发生在我身上的
都有你

All

All that has suddenly happened   I identify as you

An empty street

The wind on the face

The sun swaying in a mirror

The sudden white hair

The bee that flew into my study at 9 a.m. two days in a row

A shawl that has dropped onto the ground

The one who is leaving

And the god who is leaving

A piercing pain in the precordial area

The sharp blade that cuts my finger

The white gauze that wraps it up

The fresh blood that keeps seeping out of the gauze

All that has happened on me

Has you in it

西北风就酒

西北风就酒
没有迷途的羔羊前来问路

我们谈论一条河的宽阔清澈之于整个山河的意义
彼岸之于心灵

中年之后
我们克制着对人生长吁短叹的恶习

不再朝别人手指的方向望去
摆放神像的位置当然可以摆放木偶

你鼓掌
仅仅为了健身

真理与谬误是一场无穷无尽的诉讼
而你只有一生

时代在加速　　我们不急
自斟自饮　　偶尔也自言自语

远处的灯火有了公义的姿态却缺乏慈悲之心
我们也没有了一醉方休的豪情

浮生聚散云相似
唯有天知道

每次我赞美旅途的青山绿水
我都在想念西北高原辽阔的荒凉

To wash down the north-western wind with liquor, like the dishes

To wash down the north-western wind with liquor, like the dishes
With no stray lambs coming up to ask for directions

We are talking about the width and cleanness of a river and its meaning to
all the mountains and rivers
And the meaning of the other shore to the heart and soul

After the middle age
We refrain ourselves from the bad habit of sighing about life

And we have stopped looking in the direction that others point
Wooden effigies, of course, can also be placed where God's images are placed

You clap your hands
Only for the purpose of improving your health

True and falsehood are an endless litigation
But you only have one life

Times are speeding up   we are in no hurry
We pour ourselves a drink and drink it   and, occasionally, we talk to ourselves

Lights in the distance strike a righteous attitude but lack a kind heart
And we no longer have the passion for getting drunk, once and for all

In a floating life, gatherings and departures are like the clouds
Only heavens know

Every time I sing praise of the green mountains and waters on my journey
I miss the vast desolation of the plateau in the northwest

个人简历

使我最终虚度一生的
不会是别的
是我所受的教育　　　和再教育

C.V.

What has caused me to end up spending my life in vain

can't be anything

other than the education and re-education   I've received

云南的黄昏

云南的黄昏
我们并没谈起诗歌
夜晚也没交换所谓的苦难
两个女人
都不是母亲
我们谈论星空和康德
特蕾莎修女和心脏内科
谈论无神论者迷信的晚年
一些事物的美在于它的阴影
另一个角度：没有孩子使我们得以完整

At Dusk in Yunnan

At dusk in Yunnan
we didn't talk about poetry
nor did we exchange the so-called suffering at night
neither of us two women
was a mother
we talked about the starry skies and Kant
Mother Teresa and cardiology
about the evening years atheists were superstitious about
the beauty of certain things lay in their shadows
another angle: with no children, we ARE complete

一团白

这样的时刻　　谁
是一团白
挤过门缝里的黑夜
径直　向着你的方向

从欲望里飘出
又隐入欲望
一团痴迷的雾
在感动自己的路上
只有形状
没有重量

向着你的方向
比秘密更近
比天堂更远
在曲折的疼痛和轻声的呼唤之上
此时此刻
在苍茫的中央

A Mass of White

At such time   who
is a mass of white
the dark night, squeezing into the crack of the door
straight   in your direction

floating out of desire
before hiding in it
a mass of obsessed fog
on the way that has moved itself
with shape
but no weight

in your direction
closer than the secret
further than heavens
above tortuous pain and gentle cries
right here and now
in the centre of boundlessness

大雾弥漫

我又开始写诗　但我不知道
为什么

你好：大雾弥漫！世界已经消失
你的痛苦有了伟大的形状

请进　请参与我突如其来的写作
请见证：灵感和高潮一样不能持久

接下来是技艺　而如今
你的人生因谁的离去少了一个重要的词

你挑选剩下的：　厨房的炉火
晾衣架上的风　被修改了时间的挂钟

上个世纪的手写体：……

人间被迫熄灭的
天堂的烟灰缸旁可以继续？我做梦——

它有着人类子宫温暖的形状
将不辞而别的死再次孕育成生！

教堂已经露出了它的尖顶：
死亡使所有的痛苦都飞离了他的肉体

所有的……深怀尊严
他默然前行
一只被隐喻的蜘蛛
默默织着它的网　它在修补一场过去的大风

A Big, Pervasive Fog

I've begun writing poetry again   but I do not know
why

how are you: a big, pervasive fog! The world has disappeared
and your pain is having a great shape

please come in   to take part in my sudden writing
please witness: inspiration, like an orgasm, can't last

what follows is skills   and now
your life, because of someone's departure, is minus an important word

you choose what remains: the stove fire in the kitchen
the wind on the clothes hangers: a wall clock whose time has been revised

the hand-writing from last century: ...

can what was forcibly extinguished in the world
continue by the side of an ashtray in heavens? I have a dream—

it has the warm shape of a human womb
that turns death, leaving without a goodbye, once again into life!

the church has revealed its spire
and death has made all the pain fly away from his body

everything...with dignity deeply contained
he walks forward, in silence
a metaphorical spider
is weaving its net, in silence, too   repairing a gale of the past

干了什么

她在洗手
她一直在洗手
她一直不停地在洗手
她把手都洗出血来了
她干了什么
到底……干了什么？

What Has She Done?

She's washing her hands
She's been washing her hands
She's been washing her hands nonstop
She's washing her hands till they bleed
What has she done?
What on earth…has she done?

诗人

你有一首伟大的诗　和被它毁掉的生活
你在发言
我在看你发言

又一个
十年！

我们中间　有些人是墨水
有些人依旧像纸

春风吹着祖国的工业　农业　娱乐业
吹拂着诗歌的脸
诗人　再次获得了无用和贫穷

什么踉跄了一下
在另一个时代的眼眶　内心……

当我们握手　微笑　偶尔在山路上并肩
在伟大的春风中——
我戒了烟
你却在复吸

我正经历着一场必然的伤痛
你的婚姻也并不比前两次幸福　稳固

The Poets

You have a great poem   and its destroyed life
you are making a speech
I'm watching you make a speech

another one
10 years!

among us...some are ink
others remain like paper

The spring wind is blowing across motherland's industries   agriculture
                                   entertainment
blowing across the face of poetry
poets   once again secure uselessness and poverty

something stumbles
in the eye-socket of another age...inner heart...

when we shake hands   smile   occasionally walk shoulder by shoulder
                                   on the mountain path
in the great spring wind—
I've quit smoking
but you've resumed it

I'm experiencing a necessary pain
And your marriage is not happier   or more stable than your previous two

夜归

你带来政治和一身冷汗

嘴上颤抖的香烟　　你带来漆黑
空荡的大街

鸽子的梦话：有时候　瞬间的细节就是事情的全部！

被雨淋湿的风
几根潮湿的火柴　你带来人类对爱的一致渴望

你带来你的肉体……

多么疲惫
在她卧室的床上

Return at Night

You've brought politics and a bodyful of cold sweat

the cigarette trembling on your mouth   you've brought pitch darkness
an empty street

the dove talked in its dream: sometimes   details of a moment are the
                                                                    whole thing!

wind, wetted by the rain
a number of moistened matchsticks   you've brought a unified human
                                                                    desire for love

you've brought your flesh...

so tired
in the bed of her bedroom

西夏王陵

没有什么比黄昏时看着一座坟墓更苍茫的了
时间带来了果实却埋葬了花朵

西夏远了　贺兰山还在
就在眼前
当一个帝王取代了另一个帝王
江山发生了变化？

那是墓碑　也是石头
那是落叶　也是秋风
那是一个王朝　也是一捧黄土

不像箫　像埙——
守灵人的声音暗哑低缓：今年不种松柏了
种芍药
和牡丹

The Imperial Tombs of Western Xia

Nothing is more boundless than watching a tomb at dusk
time has brought fruit but has buried the flowers

Western Xia is distant   although the Helan Mountains are still there
right in front of my eyes
when one emperor replaced another
did the mountains and rivers change?

it's a tombstone   also a stone
it's the fallen leaves   also autumnal wind
it's a dynasty   also a handful of yellow earth

not like a Xiao, a vertical bamboo flute   more like a Xun[1]—
the vigil keeper said in a hoarse and sluggish voice: We won't plant
                                        cypresses any more
we'll plant Shaoyao
and Mudan[2]

---

1   An ancient earthen egg-shaped wind instrument, used to play music in a Confucian
shrine ceremony – translator's note.

2   Both are translated in English as 'peony' but with slight differences as the shaoyao
is shorter than the mudan. While the shaoyao is grass-based, the mudan is wood-based –
translator's note.

纸人

我用纸叠出我们
一个老了　另一个
也老了
什么都做不成了
当年　我们消耗了多少隐秘的激情

我用热气哈出一个庭院
用汪汪唤出一条小狗
用葵花唤出青豆
用一枚茶叶
唤出一片茶园
我用：喂　唤出你
比门前的喜鹊更心满意足
——在那遥远的地方

什么都做不成了
我们抽烟　喝茶　散步时亲吻——
额头上的皱纹
皱纹里的精神

当上帝认出了我们
它就把纸人还原成纸片

这样的叙述并不令人心碎
——我们商量过的：我会第二次发育　丰腴　遇见你

Paper People

I created us with a folded piece of paper
one getting old   the other
also getting old
can't do anything anymore
in those days, though, we consumed so much hidden passion

I created a courtyard by breathing out a hot breath
I called out a puppy, with a bark
I called out the green peas with sunflowers
I called out a tea garden
with a single tealeaf
and I: called you out, with a 'Hi'
more content than the magpie out at the door
—in the faraway place

can't do anything anymore
we smoked   we drunk   we kissed while taking a walk—
wrinkles on the foreheads
and spirit in the wrinkles

when God recognized us
He returned the paper people to paper pieces

such a description was not heart-breaking
—we've discussed it before: I shall develop for a second time   to become
                                    plump   and to meet you

现在

我留恋现在
暮色中苍茫的味道
书桌上的白纸
笔
表达的又一次
停顿

危险的诗行
——我渴望某种生活时陡峭的内心

Now

I miss now

the taste of boundlessness in the evening

white paper on the desk

a pen

another pause

in the expression

dangerous lines of poetry

—I desire a steep heart of hearts in a certain life

手写体

翻看旧信
我对每个手写体的你好
都答应了一声
对每个手写体的再见

仿佛真的可以再见——
废弃的铁道边
图书馆的阶梯上
歌声里的山楂树下
在肉体　对爱的
记忆里

爱了又爱
在一切的可能和最快之中……

还有谁
会在寂静的灯下
用纸和笔
为爱
写一封情书
写第二封情书……

——"你的这笔字就足以让我倾倒"
你还能对谁这么说？

Handwriting

As I went through the old letters
I replied to 'Nihao' from every style
of handwriting
and it was as if I could really bid farewell

to the farewell from every style of handwriting—
by the side of the railway in disuse
on the staircase of the library
under the hawthorn trees in the song
in the memory   of love
in the flesh

love after love
in all possibilities and the fastness...

who else is there
that can, under the still lamplight
and with paper and pen
write a love letter
and another one
for love

—'your handwriting is enough to turn me on'
who else can you say this to now?

交谈

你不会只觉得它是一次简单的呼吸
你同时会觉得它是一只手
抽出你肉体里的忧伤
给你看
然后　放回去
还是你的

你甚至觉得它是一个梦
让你在远离了它的现场
侧身
想哭

可我怎么能遏制它迅速成为往事啊

A Conversation

You won't just find it a simple breathing
you, at the same time, will feel that it's a hand
that brings sadness out of your body
and show it to you
before   putting it back in
still yours

you even feel that it's a dream
that makes you turn on your side
want to cry
when you are far away from its site

but how can I prevent it from quickly becoming a thing of the past

跳舞吧

我存在
和这世界纠缠在一起

我邀请你的姿态谦恭而优雅
我说： 跳舞吧
在月光里

慢慢
弯曲

在
月光里

月光已经很旧了
照耀却更沉　更有力

我在回忆　在慢慢
想起

你拥着我　从隔夜的往事中
退出

Let's Dance

I exist
entangled with this world

the way I invite you is modest and elegant
I say: Let's dance
in the moonlight

slowly
bending

in the
moonlight

which has been very much used
but its shine more heavy   more powerful

I'm reminiscing   slowly
recalling

how you held me   to retreat from
a thing of the past the previous night

在时间的左边

是劳动的间歇
或一年中的好时光就要过去
画布上的女人们
在时间的左边
晾晒着酒枣香气的身体

这样的香气里
有没有游丝般隐秘的哀愁?

在微醉的群山和哗哗的流水之间
在往昔与未来的风口
因劳动和幸福而得到锻炼的双乳——它的美
一点也不显得奢侈
和浪费

呵　　好时光
一轮好太阳
在它就要消失的时候
竟怀着对女人和流水的歉疚

On the Left Side of Time

is an interval of labour
or the best time of the year is about to pass
women on the canvass
on the left side of time
are sunning their bodies giving forth smells of liquor-saturated dates

in such fragrances
is there sorrow, with secrets like gossamers?

between the slightly drunken hills and splashing running waters
and in the mouth of wind between the past and the future
breasts, exercised by labour and happiness—their beauty
doesn't seem extravagant and wasteful
at all

ah,   good times
the disc of a good sun
before it's about to disappear
it feels guilty for women and flowing waters

抑郁

她给患抑郁症的丈夫带来了童话
她用童声朗读着它
她带来雪花的笑声
蜜蜂的甜蜜
带来魔术师的手臂
在消毒水气味的春天里
她用身体里的母性温暖着他
在他抑郁的身体上
造了一百个欢悦的句子
花落了又开
春去了又来
泪水漫过她的腰
在消毒水气味的春天里
在一棵香椿树下
她像知识分子那样
低声抽泣——
而这一切
并不能缓解他的抑郁

Depression

She brought a fairytale to her husband suffering from depression

she read it aloud, in a child's voice

she brought the laughter of snowflakes

the sweetness of bees

she brought the arms of a magician

in a spring smelling of disinfectant water

she warmed him up with the motherliness in her body

she made a hundred happy sentences

over his depressed body

flowers fell and re-opened

the spring went and came again

tears rose above her waist

in the spring smelling of disinfected water

under a Chinese toon tree

she, like an intellectual

was sobbing, in a low voice—

but nothing she did

could lessen his depression

下午

又一个下午过去了
我人生的许多下午这样过去——
烟在手上
书在膝上或地上
我在摇椅里
天意在天上
中年的平静在我脸上　肩上　突然的泪水里：
自然　你的季节所带来的一切　于我都是果实

Afternoon

Another afternoon has just gone
many afternoons in my life were gone, like that—
cigarette in my hand
book on my lap or on the floor
I'm sitting in a rocking chair
the meaning of the sky in the sky
quietness of middle age on my face   my shoulders   in the sudden tears:
nature   everything your seasons have brought   all fruit for me

说谎者

他在说谎
用缓慢深情的语调

他的语言湿了　眼镜湿了　衬衣和领带也湿了
他感动了自己
——说谎者
在流泪

他手上的刀叉桌上的西餐地上的影子都湿了
谎言
在继续

女人的眼睛看着别处：
让一根鱼刺卡住他的喉咙吧

The Liar

He's telling lies
in a tone that is slow and deeply felt

his language is sodden   his glasses sodden   his shirt and tie also sodden
he has moved himself
—the liar
is shedding tears

his knife and fox the Western food on the table and the shadow on the floor
                                                                    all sodden
his lies
are continuing

the woman's eyes are looking elsewhere:
let a fishbone get stuck in his throat

眺望

风云从苍白转向暗红
在窗前迂回

炉火熄灭了
一堆冷却的铁
和背过脸的裸体
仍维持着烘烤的姿态
倚窗眺望的女人
她的紫色乳房
高过诱惑
装满遗忘

她看见了时间也不能看见的

Watching

The wind and the cloud are turning from pale to a dark red
becoming circuitous around the window

the fire died down in the fireplace
a heap of iron gone cold
and nudes with their faces turned back
still maintaining the posture of getting warm by the fire
the woman leaning against the window and watching
her purple breasts
higher than seduction
filled with forgetfulness

she has seen what time can't see

阳光照旧了世界

弥漫的黄昏与一本合上的书
使我恢复了幽暗的平静

与什么有关　　多年前　　我尝试着
说出自己
——在那些危险而陡峭的分行里
他们说：这就是诗歌

那个封面上的人——他等我长大……
如今　　他已是无边宇宙中不确定的星光
和游走的尘土
哲学对他
已经毫无用处

品尝了众多的词语
曾经背叛
又受到了背叛
这一切　　独特又与你们的相同　　类似？

阳光照旧了世界
我每天重复在生活里的身体
是一堆时间的灰烬　　还是一堆隐秘的篝火

或者　　渴望被命名的事物和它的愿望带来的耻辱？

幽暗中　　我又看见了那个适合预言和占卜的山坡
他是一个人
还是一个神：
你这一生　　注定欠自己一个称谓：母亲

The Sun Made the World Old in Its Shine

The pervasive evening and a closed book
helped me recover a somber quietness

having to do with what   many years ago   when I tried to
speak myself out
—in those dangerous and steep lines
they said: but that's poetry

the one on the cover—he's waiting for me to grow up
now   he's but the uncertain starlight in the boundless universe
and a drifted dust
philosophy of no use to him
any more

having tasted many words
having betrayed
and been betrayed
all that   unique and the same as you   or similar?

The sun made the world old in its shine
my body repeated in life every day
is but a heap of time's ashes   or a heap of mysterious bonfire

or   desiring for the named things and the shame its hope can bring?

in the gloom   I saw the mountain slope fitting for prophesies and for divination
is he a person
or a deity:
you, for the rest of your life   are determined to owe yourself a title: Mother

我梦见了金斯伯格

我梦见了金斯伯格
他向我讲述垮掉的生活
缓慢　宁静　越来越轻

时间让生命干枯
让嚎叫变哑
金斯伯格没有了弹性

格林威治正是早晨
白雪和鸽子
飞上了教堂

我梦见
我们是两本书
在时间的书架上
隔着那么多的书
他最后的声音译成中文是说：
别跟你的身体作对

I Dreamt of Ginsberg

I dreamt of Ginsberg
he told me of his life as a beatnik
slowness   quietness   the getting lighter and lighter

time exhausted life
making the howling hoarse
so that Ginsberg lost his elasticity

it's just morning in Greenwich
when white snow and the doves
were flying onto the church

in my dream
we were two books
on the shelf of time
separated by so many other books
his final voice, when translated into Chinese, was:
don't pit against your own body

确认

那是月光
那是草丛
那是我的身体   我喜欢它和自然在一起

鸟儿在山谷交换着歌声
我们交换了手心里的野草莓

那是湿漉漉的狗尾巴草   和它一抖一抖的
小绒毛   童年的火柴盒
等来了童年的萤火虫?

哦那就是风   它来了
树上的叶子你挨挨我   我碰碰你
只要还有树
鸟儿就有家

那是大雾中的你
你中有我?

那是我们复杂的人类相互确认时的惊恐和迟疑
漫长的叹息……就是生活

生活是很多东西!

而此刻   生活是一只惊魂未定的蜘蛛
慌不择路
它对爱说了谎?

To confirm

That is moonlight
That is clusters of grass
That is my body   I like it to be with nature

That birds are exchanging songs in the valley
That we have exchanged the wild strawberries in the hearts of our hands

That is wet dog-tail grass   and its shivering
Fluff   matchboxes of childhood
Waiting till the fireflies of childhood come?

Oh, that's wind   it's coming
The leaves are nestling against each other   you and me
As long as there are trees
There are homes for the birds

That is you in the big fog
Am I in you?

That is the fear and uncertainty when we complicated humans mutually confirm
A long sigh   that is life

That life is many things!

And now   life is but a restless spider
That would choose any path in its panic
Did it tell lies to love?

哪一只手

这只手直截了当
这只手把每一分钟都当成
最后的时刻
这只手干得干净　　漂亮
——气流　　风　　玻璃的反光
为这只手侧身让路
并帮它稳住了一只瓷瓶

月光在窗外晃来晃去
像是在梦境里搜索
这一只手
是哪一只手？

Which Hand?

This hand was straightforward
this hand treated every minute
as the last one
this hand did a clean   pretty job
—the airflow   the wind   the reflection on the window
made way for this hand
and helped it steady a china bottle

the moonlight was swaying, from side to side, outside the window
as if searching in a dream
this hand
which hand?

聊斋的气味

一件巴黎飞来的大衣把我带进了更凛冽的冬天
威斯忌加苏打的颜色
聊斋的气味
纸上芭蕾的轻柔
痛苦削瘦着我的腰

肉体消失了　爱情
在继续？

——聊斋的气味
它使黑夜动荡
使所有的雪花都迷失了方向
使时间　突然
安静下来

我把脸埋在手里
像野花把自己凋零在郊外

一件巴黎飞来的大衣
把我带进更浓烈的酒杯　偶尔的
粗话

让我想想……

让我像一团雾
或一团麻　那样
想想

The Smell of Liaozhai[1]

An overcoat that flew from Paris took me into a colder winter
the colour of whisky and soda
the smell of Liaozhai
the softness of ballet on paper
when pain thinned my waist

the body was disappearing   love
still continuing?

— the smell of Liaozhai
that made the night restless
and that disoriented all the snowflakes
that caused time   to go suddenly
quiet

I buried my face in my hands
like the wild flowers that were withering themselves in the outskirts of the city

an overcoat that flew from Paris
took me to a stronger glass of wine   an occasional
rude remark

let me think

let me think
like a mass of fog
or a mass of ma (hemp)

---

1   'Liaozhai' has no matching equivalent in English as it's half of the title from the
famous novel by Pu Songling, *Liaozhai zhiyi*, which was translated as *Strange Stories
from a Chinese Studio*.

母亲

黄昏。雨点变小
我和母亲在小摊小贩的叫卖声中
相遇
还能源于什么
母亲将手中最鲜嫩的青菜
放进我的菜篮

母亲！

雨水中最亲密的两滴
在各自飘回自己的生活之前
在白发更白的暮色里
母亲站下来
目送我

像大路目送着她的小路
母亲——

Mother

At dusk. Raindrops were becoming smaller
mother and I were meeting
amidst street peddlers crying their wares
what else could this have stemmed from
mother put the freshest vegetables in her hand
in my vegetable basket

Mother!

the two most intimate raindrops in the rain
before they drifted back to their own lives
and in the colours of dusk when white hair was whiter
mother stood
and watched me leave

like a big road watching her little path
mother—

如果

如果暮色中的这一切还源于爱情——

手中的蔬菜
路边的鲜花
正在配制的钥匙
问路人得到的方向
一只灰鸟穿过飞雪时的鸣叫
一个人脚步缓慢下来时的内心

——冷一点　　又有何妨
如果这一切都在抵达着夜晚的爱情

If

If all of this at dusk comes from love originally—

vegetables in hand
roadside flowers
keys that are being cut
directions gained from a passer-by
the calling of a bird that flies through the flying snow
the heart of hearts of someone whose footsteps are slowing down

—a bit cold   so what
if all of this is arriving at the love of the night

摇椅里

我慢慢摇着　慢慢
飘忽
或者睡去

还有什么是重要的！

像一次抚摸　从清晨到黄昏
我的回忆
与遗忘
既不关乎灵魂也不关乎肉体

飘忽
或者睡去
空虚或者继续空虚……

隐约的果树
已在霜冻前落下了它所有的果实
而我　仍属于下一首诗——

和它的不可知

In the Rocking Chair

I slowly rock   slowly
drifting
or falling asleep

is there anything that is important now?

like a touch   from morning till dusk
my memory
and my loss of it
is neither related to soul or flesh

drifting
or falling asleep
feeling empty or continuing to feel empty...

faintly, fruit trees
have dropped all their fruit before the freezing frost
and I   still belong to the next poem—

and its unknownableness

我知道

我知道——整个下午她都在重复这句话

掩饰着她的颤抖　　耻辱
她的一无所知

咖啡杯开始倾斜
世界在晃

"你知道　我比你更爱他的身体……"

是的
我……知道

她希望自己能换一句话
等于这句话
或者说出这句话：
请允许我用沉默
维护一下自己的尊严吧

她希望能克制这样的眼前——
从生活的面前绕到了生活的背后

I Know

I know—she's been repeating this all afternoon

covering up her tremble   her shame
her ignorance

the coffee cup began tilting
the world shaking

'you know   I love his body more than you...'

yes
I...know

she was hoping she could replace something
equivalent to that remark
or said something like this:
please let me use silence
keep my dignity

she was hoping to restrain the moment—
encircling life by moving from the front of life to its back

忏悔

——宽恕我吧
我的肉体　　这些年来
我亏待了你

我走在去教堂的路上

用我的红拖鞋　　用我的灯笼裤
腰间残留的
夜色

蛐蛐和鸟儿都睡着了
我还在走
所有的尘埃都落定了
我还在走

天空平坦
而忏悔陡峭

我走在去教堂的路上
崇高爱情使肉体显得虚幻
我的起伏是轻微的
我的忧郁也并未因此得到缓解

A Confession

—Forgive me
my flesh   for these many years
I have not been treating you well

I'm on my way to a church

with my red slippers   with my bloom pants
and the colours of the night
that remain around my waist

the crickets and the birds are all asleep
I am still walking
all the dust has settled
I am still walking

the sky is flat
but the confession is steep

I am on my way to the church
sublime love makes the flesh illusory
my heaving is slight
and my sadness is not lessened because of this

聊天室

一个资产拥有者在抽烟　　喝茶　玩打火机
咳嗽时　　摸一下给市场经济
下过跪的双膝
他再一次强调：拒绝任何形式的回忆

我们的评论家　　在批判一只鸟：
从民间的树杈向政府大楼的飞行中
这只鸟彻底完成了立场的转换
它的叫声
是可疑的
必须警惕

我喜欢的诗人　　他们叫她
女诗人：
我被告之朗诵
就是说　我必须公开发表一次
我的脸蛋　三围　我新衣服里的旧身体

一个农药时代的菜农　　正在努力表达
喜欢你以后……
他陷入了语言的沼泽地
每一次用力
都意味着更深的绝望

The Chatroom

An owner of capital is smoking   drinking tea   playing with a cigarette-
                                                    lighter
when he coughs   he touches the knees
knelt for the market economy
he keeps stressing: Rejecting memory of any form

our critics   are criticizing a bird:
in its flight from the fork of a tree trunk among the commoners to the
                                            government building
the bird has thoroughly completed the change of her position
her calls
are suspicious
that one must be vigilant about

the poet I like   they call her
a woman poet:
I'm told to give a reading
that is to say   I must publicly publish for once
my face   my three dimensions   my old body in the new clothes

a vegetable grower in an age of pesticide   is trying to express
after liking you…
he sank into the marshland of language
every strenuous effort
means deeper despair

正是这个菜农
最后对互联网说:
再新鲜的语言也抵不过一把具体的菠菜

他的鹅毛笔一直在晃　是写童话的安徒生:
大雪已经落下
奇迹并没出现
卖火柴的小女孩全白了
在新年的钟声敲响之前
我必须让她哭泣的舌头　舔在我文字的
奶油蛋糕上

it is this same vegetable grower

who said to the internet:

the freshest language is not as good as a handful of concrete spinach

his quill has been swaying   it's Anderson the writer of fairytales

the big snow has fallen

no miracle has appeared

the little match girl is all white

before the clock strikes for New Year

I must let her weeping tongue   lick the cream cake

of my words

www.ingramcontent.com/pod-product-compliance
Lightning Source LLC
Chambersburg PA
CBHW030846090426
42737CB00009B/1122